IT'S TIME TO BAKE APRICOT SESAME COOKIES

It's Time to Bake APRICOT SESAME COOKIES

Walter the Educator

Silent King Books
A WhichHead Entertainment Imprint

Copyright © 2025 by Walter the Educator

All rights reserved. No part of this book may be reproduced in any manner whatsoever without written per- mission except in the case of brief quotations embodied in critical articles and reviews.

First Printing, 2025

Disclaimer

This book is a literary work; the story is not about specific persons, locations, situations, and/or circumstances unless mentioned in a historical context. Any resemblance to real persons, locations, situations, and/or circumstances is coincidental. This book is for entertainment and informational purposes only. The author and publisher offer this information without warranties expressed or implied. No matter the grounds, neither the author nor the publisher will be accountable for any losses, injuries, or other damages caused by the reader's use of this book. The use of this book acknowledges an understanding and acceptance of this disclaimer.

It's Time to Bake APRICOT SESAME COOKIES is a collectible early learning book by Walter the Educator suitable for all ages belonging to Walter the Educator's Time to Bake Book Series. Collect more books at WaltertheEducator.com

USE THE EXTRA SPACE TO TAKE NOTES AND DOCUMENT YOUR MEMORIES

APRICOT SESAME COOKIES

It's baking time, come gather near,

It's Time to Bake Apricot Sesame Cookies

Apricot sesame cookies bring us cheer!

Soft and sweet with a nutty crunch,

Perfect for snacks or an afternoon munch.

First, we'll gather what we need,

Flour, butter, and sugar indeed.

Apricots dried, so soft and bright,

And sesame seeds, golden and light.

Mix the butter, creamy and smooth,

Add sugar to sweeten the mood.

In goes an egg, then stir with glee,

This dough is as fun as it can be!

Sift the flour, light as air,

Add a pinch of salt with care.

Sprinkle sesame seeds like little pearls,

Stirring gently, let's give it swirls.

It's Time to Bake Apricot Sesame Cookies

Now chop the apricots, tiny and sweet,

Bits of sunshine we're ready to meet.

Fold them into the dough just so,

It's starting to look like a cookie show!

Scoop the dough into little mounds,

Round and golden, they'll astound!

Place them neatly, row by row,

On a baking tray, ready to go.

Pop them in the oven to bake,

The kitchen smells like a warm embrace.

Golden sesame, apricot sweet,

Oh, what a lovely, delicious treat!

Ding, ding, ding! The cookies are done,

They're golden brown, oh what fun!

Let them cool for just a bit,

It's Time to Bake
Apricot Sesame Cookies

Before we take our very first bite.

Soft and chewy with sesame's crunch,

Perfect for breakfast or after lunch.

Share with friends or save a few,

There's plenty for all, it's up to you!

Baking cookies is such a delight,

With apricots and sesame shining bright.

So grab your apron, let's bake once more,

It's Time to Bake
Apricot Sesame Cookies

New memories and cookies galore!

ABOUT THE CREATOR

Walter the Educator is one of the pseudonyms for Walter Anderson. Formally educated in Chemistry, Business, and Education, he is an educator, an author, a diverse entrepreneur, and he is the son of a disabled war veteran.
"Walter the Educator" shares his time between educating and creating. He holds interests and owns several creative projects that entertain, enlighten, enhance, and educate, hoping to inspire and motivate you. Follow, find new works, and stay up to date with Walter the Educator™

at WaltertheEducator.com